FEASTING & FORAGING

A COLLECTION OF ESSAYS ON HOPE AND FOOD

CYNTHIA M. STUCKEY

Photos courtesy of Leah Janik, Lumarie Photo & Design

Edited by Kate Motaung, Refine Services

For Lance,
my favorite barista & sous chef,
wherever you are, I am at home.

FEASTING & FORAGING

CONTENTS

Home is never simply a threshold you cross. It is a place you make and a place that might make — or unmake — you.

— CHRISTIE PURIFOY, PLACEMAKER

1

FORAGING AND FINDING

L ance and I honeymooned at the North Carolina State
Farmers Market.

ACTUALLY, we honeymooned in Mexico, but the idea of actually
beginning our real life together was so enticing to me that I
dragged him downtown to buy local produce just after we came
home—sunburnt and full of Tacos Al Pastor.

A SHORT DRIVE into Raleigh delivered rows of pickup trucks
backed up to open air stalls, all offering their goods. The buzz
of people and the scent of muscadine grapes greeted us as we
began what would become our weekly saunter from one end of
the covered building to the other. Saturday mornings at the
market became the weekend ritual that shaped our cooking
and eating and thus, our brand new life.

. . .

OUR FIRST FALL together was studded with dishes like butternut squash risotto and salads with nectarines and goat cheese. Together, we learned how to make chard that was not a punishment to eat, and how to properly roast a chicken. Dinner was served at our coffee table most nights (scandalous) with the background music of Alton Brown and America's Test Kitchen educating us as we ate.

LIFE WAS A FEAST.

WE FEASTED ON TIME ITSELF, ingredients available to us, and the glistening gift of being together. Every week, a shiny new meal plan—new recipes to try and taste and then eat for three or four days. (Cooking for only two people is, after all, one of the hardest parts of newlywed life—that, and trying to get the duvet cover back on the duvet.)

NEARLY TWELVE YEARS LATER, much has changed and yet nothing has. We live in a different state altogether and we don't make it to the Farmers Market as often. I still come home with too much produce from roadside stands, and Lance still smiles and helps me rearrange the refrigerator to find a place for five pounds of zucchini.

We have grown from a couple of foodies to a family of food-lovers, though our children abhor all stinky cheeses and each appreciate an incongruous list of vegetables.

THAT AUTUMN of building our meals around what was local, seasonal, and fresh may have been an adventure of plenty, but it taught me a lesson in seeing and using what I have.

. . .

Sometimes I stand at the refrigerator and see only abundance. Peppers. Check. Leafy greens still crunchy and fresh. Check. That one good cheese from Trader Joe's that we all love. Check. Butter. Check. Check. And check.

But every now and then I stand in my kitchen to cook and discover the terrible fact that I have forgotten to purchase one important ingredient. No matter what else I do have at my disposal, I simply don't have what I need.

When my fridge is politely full I can see the potential; when I have to scrounge around a bit for the elements of dinner—well, that's where the fun lies.

Some of our greatest, most satisfying meals have been the end result of disjointed odds and ends. We all have our talents, and foraging for ingredients in the fridge might be mine. I will never be a long-distance runner, but I can take fragments and toss them together to make a really good salad—a salad that doesn't taste like leftovers. Greens, half a honey crisp apple, a bit of bacon, an ounce of leftover cheese, one sad carrot hacked off and grated until only the fresh part remains, and a handful of toasted pecans . . . add a simple vinaigrette, and boom—you have a salad that some restaurant would charge thirteen dollars for.

. . .

THE WORLD often thinks of "making do" as a negative improvisation—an act reserved for power outages and post-Depression era grandparents.

BUT I KNOW it to be a gift.

A gift that causes me to not just see what I have, but to see what God makes of my odds and ends.

THE CONCEPT OF FEASTING & Foraging is this understanding that perspective changes our vision. The disjointed pieces that don't seem like enough at first glance can actually become more than we could ask for.

OFTEN WE SEE what is in front of us and there is only abundance. The breathtaking display of God's provision and protection with a splash of extra grace sprinkled in is evident in all that we have. Like a complete Thanksgiving dinner, those are the moments we feast on hope. Hope spills over all around us, everywhere we look—like a table filled to the very edges with good things. Though we know the world is not rose-colored, at the moment, it looks that way to us.

AND THEN.

Then there are moments when we look at what we have, and it's difficult—if not impossible—to ignore the mental, physical, or emotional lack. What we thought we had, we don't have enough of; what we thought we needed, we do not see.

WE ACHE INSIDE AND OUT.

We are broken.
We are discouraged.
We are (still) waiting.
We are in need.
We are disappointed that our prayers sit unanswered.
We are foraging—for some shred of hope.

IN TRYING to reconcile what we know with what we feel, we may forget that all that is so deeply touched by grace still bears the scars of a life lived in a world marked by pain. We can recite what is true. But we often need to be reminded, to shade our perspective with the colors of what we know. We need someone to tilt our chin up toward the light, that we might see that what we stand entrenched in today is not all there is, or what will be.

GRATEFULNESS HAS the power to change what we see. With our lives, with our meals, and with every daily task, we are telling a story. We are telling a story that we have been told all our lives, through both the living Word and His Creation.

IT IS a story of His provision.

OF HIS NEVER ENDING GRACE TO and protection of His people. It is the thread of mercy that runs through history right to our kitchen doors. An ordinary meal is only ordinary when we call it so. What we often sneer at as "the best we could do" might be the best of what another would ever hope for. And perhaps every time we choose not to miss the chance to truly say "all is grace," we are reminded just how good our Father is.

. . .

GRATEFULNESS CAN BE OUR NARRATIVE. That in all we have, whether we feast or forage or struggle somewhere in between with ingredients from both, we have enough. Much like those Sunday afternoon leftover fridge clean out meals. It may look a bit strange, with someone eating leftover chicken salad while another plate has two pieces of pizza and one scoop of roasted broccoli. Our meal may appear to be puzzle pieces fitting oddly together on a dinner plate—but we came hungry, and we have eaten and been filled.

HOPE IS THAT WAY, my friend.

Perspective gives us hope lenses to look through. Lenses that shine light on what we have instead of casting shadows of doubt and frustration.

BUT HERE IS what I do know: We do not learn this lesson once. We do not purpose to cling to hope early in the morning on Monday and find it carries us long past the doldrums of Wednesday afternoon.

At least, it doesn't for me.

In a savage season of hardness, I must choose to let truth lift my chin toward hope throughout the day, often many times before noon.

WE CAN FIND joy in the forage until we feast. And then feast until we feel another forage coming our way.

It is the dance of want and plenty that keeps us twirling from gratefulness to supplication and back again. We need both the days of feasting and the days of foraging to remind us of our longing. Just as it is a particular kind of delight to step back and see God provide for an abject need we've had for so long, it is the same with cooking from sparse ingredients.

THE FOOD really isn't ever the point. It is a vehicle for togetherness, joy, and provision. Feeding others has always been a moniker of life and creativity for me and I cannot look around at the prismatic colors of what God has given us in nature and not praise Him.

AND SOMETIMES, I most need to praise Him when it is the most difficult.

When the furthest thing from my bruised heart is to celebrate my abundance, I need the thread that runs down the middle of my kitchen table and reminds me of how I have been cared for.

I NEED to start with what I know and go from there.

Even if it is one sentence of truth. One verse of God's Word, whispered to and from my soul again and again throughout the static of a regular day.

ONE FOUND ingredient in the back of my freezer, one perfectly grilled chicken breast waiting to adorn a big salad, a pizza, or a sheet pan of nachos that we will all love.

IT IS NEVER JUST AN INGREDIENT—IT'S a reminder of what we have been given in love from the God Who Sees, a small component of what will become—a feast.

A LETTER TO OUR OLD KITCHEN

D ear Blue House Kitchen,
  So this is how it ends.

With crow bars and splintered wood and more drywall dust than there was snow in Narnia. There are parts of you I cannot wait to see sitting in a heap on the front lawn, like the cabinet doors we painted poorly, the ones that stuck from Day One and scuffed on Day Fourteen.

And up top, above the microwave that stopped working yesterday, where the faux brick protrudes—that is all going and I am not the least bit sad about it.

That part of the wall that has been missing trim every day of the eight-and-a-half years we have lived here? It goes. And to the cable jack, the phone jack, and the random electrical box for which we never knew the purpose—I say adieu and good riddance.

The missing cabinets. The squeaking drawers. The countertops that warp in the summer and when we use the slow cooker too many times in a week, the ones with the crack down the middle that I always cover with the toaster—they're going, too.

. . .

YOU NEED to understand something about me that you may not know in spite of our time together: I never hated you.

I was never embarrassed by you.

Sure, you were outdated and peeling and drafty, but you were mine. You held us like a hug, between the pantry and the bay window with arms of welcome and space to cook, eat, and play countless games of UNO.

The way the soft, yellow sun shines gauzy through your windows in the morning—this daily helped me to count my gifts. Even in the grayer months, when your windows revealed nothing but fog and sticky, stalky trees, I lit taper candles and loved you anyway. From Christmas morning cinnamon rolls to birthday cakes to that time we took up pasta making—all my best memories involving food, carbs, and this family— have you as the backdrop.

Your floors kept us as we danced from Boogie Shoes to Hillsong. First we were three, and then we were four. I never minded your mid-range builder-grade vinyl, not even compared to real hardwood—not when I remembered the way Abby took her first steps into Lance's arms, grinning and toddling in footie pajamas and a baby comb-over fresh from the tub as Lucy chirped and cheered her on. That is one of my favorite memories here; I think it may be one of yours, too.

Remember the times I snuck into your pantry to find a moment of peace and a piece of dark chocolate? I suppose you also remember the time I slipped inside to hold sad news and cry hot, despairing tears.

Thank you for offering solace on that hard day.

I hope you saw all the times we laughed out loud, just happy to share the food we pulled together in you. And how sweet it was to have those at-home date nights after the girls went to sleep, with Drew Holcomb playing low as we made guacamole and fridge forager nachos in our bare feet. We have lived a contented life with you as our culinary setting. Years of meals made and prayers said here, earnestly, desperately, gratefully—for ourselves and for the ones we love.

In you we made a family and a love and you, Blue House kitchen, have held just about the entire history of us as parents here between your windows, so you may be wondering why all the ruckus and men walking in and out and preparing to tear you apart.

It's not personal . . . it's water damage.

A tiny leak caused a huge problem and led to what the professionals call "a kitchen overhaul."

And well, to be honest, we have always wanted to spruce you up a bit, but because of the extent of the damage, it seems you are going to get a full fresh start. Oh, and you can trust that kind lady with the tape measure and the clipboard. She knows how much we love you and we rely on her to keep your heart intact.

I was careful to pick things that I knew you would like. Shades that bring even more light to shine on top of the girls' heads as they eat breakfast and again as they play Legos in the late afternoon.

Don't worry about the shiny new granite—it will be just as serviceable as the old countertops. More cabinets, deeper drawers, the kind that don't slam or pinch tiny fingers. We're not leaving you behind, just giving you some new clothes.

It's going to be beautiful, and well, you know us—we are excited about the chance to love what we have; to love where we live— just a little bit more. And really, these months of living with a plywood floor have reminded me how much I would love to make coffee in my bare feet again.

BUT BEFORE IT ALL BEGINS, before the banging, splitting, hammering, and drilling, I just needed you to know—I was truly happy cooking for my little family in my original, imperfect, Blue House kitchen.

No matter how our hearts swell with the fresh and updated, all glittering and brand new—none of it will diminish how irrevocably settled we have always been within your walls.

And no matter what, I promise not to love your glossy, gleaming, new things so much that I ever forget how incandescently happy we were in the days of chipped paint, well-loved, and quite comfortably broken in.

You were (almost nearly) perfect.

JAPANESE ICED COFFEE

The recipe for Japanese Iced Coffee should come factory direct with every newborn baby, alongside those really gauzy muslin blankets.

JAPANESE ICED COFFEE is not nearly as fancy as it sounds, but is simply brewing hot coffee over ice, resulting in an Iced Coffee which is immediately ready for consumption, unlike other methods— such as cold brew— which can take up to 24 hours to prepare. This method, which can be made in less than five minutes results in perfectly cool, strong coffee when you need it most. And let's be honest, knowing I can run home and have a glass of this ready in five minutes has saved me billions of dollars at the coffee shop drive thru.

Provisions.

One Kettle for boiling water, (or in a pinch, boil water however and use a glass measuring cup to pour carefully.)

One Pour-over coffee pot with filter. (We use a Chemex with cotton/paper filters, but any pour-over device will do.)

Coffee, freshly ground if possible.

Water + Ice

For Two Servings.

(a small 2-cup, such as a Hario)

40 grams of coffee or 1/2 cup

400 grams of water or 2 cups

200 grams of ice or 1 heaping cup

For Three- Four Servings.

(a standard size Chemex pot)

60 grams of coffee or 3/4 cup

600 grams of water or 2 1/2 cups

400 grams of ice or 2 cups

METHOD.

Place ice in the bottom of the pour-over pitcher. Then slowly pour the boiling water over the coffee grounds. As the hot water drips through, the ice will melt. Allow the coffee 90 seconds to complete the drip process. Discard the filter/ coffee grounds and pour cool coffee over additional ice and serve however. I like a splash of cream, and on occasion, a dash of maple or simple syrup.

3

CAPE TOWN

As an eight-year-old holding a new book, my fingers fanned forward and I devoured the last three pages first. It drove my mom crazy and she would deny me new books until I promised to stop. At thirty-six I practice restraint, but I am still that girl. I want to know that everything turns out all right before I invest myself in the characters.

I am an annoying optimist on a relentless hunt for hope. The more I face the darkness, the more I arch my back and refuse to see only brokenness. In every desperate situation, I crave redemption. The Enneagram pegs me firmly as a number nine with a one wing. Basically I am your worst kind of Pollyanna-with-a-strong-streak-of-sense-of-rightness nightmare.

But sometimes the struggle to always see the sunshine is a weakness.

Often my ache to see restoration keeps me from plumbing the depths of someone's pain—or even my own.

For the last three Februarys, I have crammed too many things into a large suitcase and joined a ministry team in Cape Town, South Africa. We go to see specific women, names and smiles we know well. Women who mother bravely amidst a harder reality than I have ever known. They hold a large chunk of my heart.

Even the city itself is a juxtaposition of beauty and brokenness.

A staggering paradox of rippling turquoise water teeming with life contrasts with dry, hot sand—a clear picture of the extremes of South Africa. I breathe the briny air and brace myself. My internal dialogue is one of stoicism and bravery: Be strong this time. You've seen this before. Pull it together.

But deep inside, I hear a whisper and it calls me back to a place of dependence, not resilience. Strong is not always the goal.

WE SIT TOGETHER. These women from the southern tip of Africa elbow to elbow with us; we have much in common. The Cape Town breeze lifts their voices higher as they share their stories with us. It has been a year since we have been together but they remember the song; they sing with us, around us, and over us.

It is in this moment when the wind picks up and storm clouds peek over the mountains that I know the lump in my throat is there to stay. These women, who haven't had rain or water to waste for months and months, sing loud and with their whole bodies. They sing in a language I do not speak but that joy, the way they sing with their faces upturned? That joy is a friend to me. And yet I am unsure I could sing so loudly in such a time of uncertainty. But they do—and I am the one being ministered to. Light raindrops begin to fall on our faces and forearms. I do not brush away even one drop, but let each one soak into my skin.

. . .

LATER WE TALK of God's goodness and provision and they tell poignant stories of how He has met them. Words of assent and praise dance off the walls like refracted light. As we listen to one another, the language obstacle seems irrelevant. There is no barrier here and I do not even try to explain it. I never want to forget this, finding sisters more than seven thousand miles from my own front porch.

And this is the gift—not a gift that we bring but that God gives us in them.

That entering into another's suffering builds space for sharing in another's joy. There is hope here and it is plentiful. It abounds not in spite of all they have walked through, but because they know who has walked them through it. I think, just maybe, I miss the depth of the hope when I rush to skip over the depth of the sorrow.

THERE IS RARELY a time we are not called to compassion but sometimes I need my heart shattered into a thousand tiny shards to see the depth of another's suffering. It hurts. It is not my own personal brand of pain to know details that may keep me staring at the ceiling later when I should be sleeping.

But I need to know it. The anguish makes the redemption something we all need. Until our Maker makes everything broken to be broken no more, we have to keep stepping in.

JUST BEFORE WE leave Cape Town and turn our hearts toward home, our van speeds by one of the poorest and most dangerous townships in the city. I have heard stories of the terror within and I want to pull my eyes to the road ahead of us, focused on the journey home. Instead, my chin juts to the left, face to face with it all—expecting to receive one last souvenir of sadness I cannot fix.

Row after row of tiny buildings, people huddled together. One dismal, central water source and a line snaking up to it.

Then I saw him. A small boy about my Lucy's age. Dancing. Running and jumping in a crazy obstinance to the brokenness around him. The writer in me hungered to know more—to know why he was dancing. Was it something insignificant that moved his little body in opposition to the sadness?

Or was he just . . . happy?

In that moment, it was enough to see a glimpse of hope. To be reminded that God Himself, His very presence, is in the most horrifying of places. Those places we wish did not exist, places that seethe with evil. Where there is one of His creatures in need of Him, He is there. When all of the world seems to ache with destruction, He is artfully at work in the dark and quiet places in ways we may never see.

BACK HOME, I turn this fact over and over again in my mind. I sift through the last eleven days and remember all that was good and hard. If I pause long enough to look out from where I stand in the southern part of North America, I see this same glittering hope all around me.

Hope glistens in front of me as my friend recalls the first photo of her youngest son, laying in an orphanage bed. In need. Now he is all smiles and snacks and superheroes. His parents saved their pennies and sold t-shirts and avoided vacations and all manner of luxuries to afford adoption fees. He has a name and it is theirs and I think only of the gospel when he runs up and gives me an unprompted bear hug.

Hope shines in the voice of another friend who gives up her comfort daily to fight injustice. Righteously, passionately opposed to the evil in the world and not afraid to help others see what they miss in their comfort. She fights an unpopular battle for the marginalized and her voice is one that God uses to shake me awake on a regular basis.

Other places, hope is less vocal, less obvious, but shining and refracting just the same.

All around me floats this same luminous hope and I see it more clearly when I allow myself to enter in. To dance with the anguish before squinting to see only the joy.

I am better equipped to be a light bringer when I acknowledge the depth of the darkness and when I remember that the darkness will never win.

Together, you and I must turn and look deeply when we want to look away and settle our eyes on lovelier things. We may crave happier, lighter stories shaded yellow like sunshine, but we balance our hunger for rightness with the knowledge that many cannot choose to avoid the hurt. A large portion of the world we live in is full of faces that live daily in the city of pain. Still in the deeper, darker anguish there is loveliness to be found. Because what could be more lovely than the renovation that only comes as a result of new life?

What could captivate us more than a life changed completely by the gospel we know so well?

What could make us more reliant than not being able to hold all the joy and all the pain we know and see and touch?

What could be more beautiful than knowing it will not always be like this?

Nothing.

AFFOGATO

It may seem odd to equate this dessert masquerading as an Italian coffee drink with South Africa, but stick with me. During one particularly long day in Cape Town, my friend Trish and I had to run a glamorous errand— it involved the South African version of a dollar store and buying bath towels in neon colors, which would prove to be a mistake— as the colors ran the minute they got wet.

On our way back, we spotted a roadside sign with a few glorious words— *Coffee Roaster This Way.*

After the beautiful but long day we had, this place was basically Aslan's Country. Terbadore Coffee held a glistening espresso machine, large shining jars of rusks and cookies, and a patio garden. We bought two take away dirty chai's without a second thought and continued down the road. Once our cups were lightweight and growing cold, we both realized that we had forgotten to even think of bringing coffee to our other team members. Oops. Luckily, they forgave us when we took them back the next day.

.   .   .

THE FOLLOWING AFTERNOON, we sat at a long wooden table with backless benches. My friend Jacqueline ordered an affogato and it was the prettiest one I have ever seen. Affogato, or *drowned*, in Italian is a lovely decadence and if you have never had the pleasure— well, you're welcome.

There is some discussion over whether Affogato is a coffee drink or a dessert. I think the hot fudge absolutely gives it dessert status but if you want to drink it as coffee, I support you.

~

PROVISIONS.
Hot Fudge (directions to make your own below)
Hot Espresso 1oz.
Vanilla Bean Ice Cream or Gelato

SIMPLE HOT FUDGE.
3 oz. Bittersweet chocolate, chopped
1/4 cup of unsalted butter
One can of sweetened condensed milk
Tiny pinch of salt
Combine all ingredients in a heavy-bottomed sauce pan over medium heat. Stir consistently until it melts and has a beautiful, glossy sheen. Pour into a jar with a lid and serve soon after.

. . .

DIRECTIONS.

In a small juice glass, (I love the IKEA ones— and their tiny spoons are perfect with this.) Smear hot fudge around the inside of the glass. Add a good, healthy scoop of ice cream. If you have enough shot glasses (unless you spent your college years at a seminary like I did. I only have two shot glasses, and they've only ever held espresso,) serve the shot of hot espresso on the side of the ice cream/ fudge mixture and allow your guests to pour it on at the very last moment.

Buon appetito!

∾

4

MY PARENTS' DAUGHTER

Last spring, we turned a corner in our family.
The first grandchild, my oldest brother's only daughter, married a good, kind man. Their wedding day was the only non-sweltering Saturday that March. The sky and the St. John's River blended together in the same shade of hopeful blue.

Lyndsay and Jamie's wedding day felt like a sweet production in which we all played a part. My mom baked a spectacular cake that renewed our faith in how delicious a wedding cake could be—vanilla with raspberry filling and buttercream light enough to float away on. One of my brothers officiated the ceremony. Another stayed awake all night with our dad to smoke enough barbecue for an army. They slid into the church pew minutes before the processional wearing tired eyes and the scent of hickory on their hair from a night of mastering the grill.

Several of the bridesmaids had been the flower girls in my own wedding over a decade earlier. I remembered them with frilly dresses and sweet smiles, pulling up itchy tights in August. Now they are gorgeous young women—confident and strong. They stood on pieces of blue painter's tape to mark their spots and beamed at their cousin as she swept down the center aisle with her dad. My big brother grinned from his beard to his earlobes. I squeezed Lance's hand and tried not to cry.

Noteworthy and whimsical, this particular wedding had us all reminiscing. The bride was the first swaddled bundle I ever held at the age of nine; the first baby I treasured. That day she was the first grandchild to become someone's wife.

All day my eyes threatened to spill over at the knowledge that time was rushing past all around us. I snapped mental photos of my nieces and nephews and laid them next to other pictures in my mind; pictures of when all these big kids, now adults, were the tiny ones I remembered. As I watched them smiling in silk and tuxedos, I could not help but see them running through the sprinkler at ages five, six, and seven. All these memories sit right next to my stack of even older grainy Polaroids from when their dads and I were that little. When we were the "Blythe kids" running pell-mell around the family gathering and playing Capture the Flag in the pitch black backyard.

Wasn't it just last year that we all did homework around the dining room table while waiting for the dinnertime doorbell signaling the delivery of our Friday night pizza?

I am fairly certain that a few short weeks ago we colored eggs and hid them in the bushes in the front yard after church.

But no.

It has been years and the children of the children who ran around with Easter baskets and earless chocolate bunnies now stand between five and six feet tall, huddled together and laughing at a common joke.

As WEDDINGS OFTEN DO, this day held the beauty of a fresh beginning but with occasional notes of a family and her history. It caused me to stop and see what I miss in the daily dance of fixing snacks and braiding hair. The entire day made me soberly aware of what we have in one another.

For all our change, growing up and multiplying has not made us anything but closer together. New pieces of us have been added by marriages and births—lots of births, actually. My parents had a bumper crop of kids and grandkids. From the outside, from the Facebook photos of all of us smiling, it might seem like nothing but days of sunshine have ever graced our family.

BUT IF YOU HAVE A FAMILY, even a fiercely inseparable one, then you know. You know that though our face-stretching grins in those photos are very real, so are the other moments.

We have known the fear of big dangers. We have woken in the inky black of night with each other to pray as we wait for morning and good news.

We have held broken hearts.

We have prayed for babies. We have praised God when He healed them, and felt grief when He did not heal them in the way we asked.

We have not always known how to love each other, not always known how to tell each other hard things. We have not always known how to keep each other tethered to where we truly should be.

We have made mistakes.

But God.

God has kept us close; He has kept us a family. When we gather around a table of ribs and five half-empty bottles of barbecue sauce, the sweetness of our time together is bigger somehow because we know we simply do not get the credit for this gift.

God has done this work in us. He has brought us together time and again when the unthinkable happens. In joy and in grief. We have said farewell to our grandparents, one by one, together. Always together, moving down the line of folding tables that sag under casseroles and cakes. Together in the church pew, singing Amazing Grace and remembering it to be Grandpa's favorite hymn, one he lived out. We mark our years in Thanksgivings and Fourth of July barbecues and regular Sunday lunches that feel like a holiday—simply because we are together.

AT ONE POINT during the wedding reception last March, the photographer corralled us and all our offspring outside for a picture. Stepping around tree roots, we avoided shade and anthills and clustered together. Even with a wide angle lens, we crammed to be in one photo. With my hand looped through my husband's arm, I looked back to see both of our girls mixed in the happy jumble of their cousins. To the side, my oldest brother smiling at his oldest daughter, in white. My parents, somewhere in the center, beaming to have us all sharing a patch of grass. All around us was the whispered hum of muttered jokes and stifled laughter bubbling out, the sound of a lifetime, the sound of a family. The echo of grace, multiplied from two parents to five children, to nineteen and counting.

And this is how love both heals and aches. To know that we had reached the point of change. We had arrived at the inter-section of child and parent, and turned a corner as a family. We had become the adults, all at once and gradually—between birthday parties and late nights around the grill, passing babies back and forth, opening each other's children's snacks, and never stopping to realize that as they were steadily getting older —so were we.

Being the baby of the family, I grew up having everyone care for me. Then I became quite disgruntled when one by one, they started to leave home and find their new grown-up lives. I had the same startling feeling when I realized my grandparents were all gone and my mom and dad were the grandparents now. The feeling came slowly to me, and last, as I am the last to grow up, the full stop.

There is an uncertainty to standing in the middle place— the place between being a child and still needing your parents as they begin to need you a bit more. Realizing that time is both a gift and a dirty, rotten thief is like finding yourself on the chairlift of a ski hill and questioning whether you spent enough time in ski school. You cannot go back. But if you go forward, you may faceplant.

YOU NEED your parents more than ever.

They will soon need you more than before.

WHEN I THINK about the next two decades of my own adult-hood, I get a lump in my throat. I am not always ready to be the adult, though I pay taxes and schedule dentist appointments for not only myself, but my own children.

I am grown. But there have been days I have held my knees tucked under my chin as I called my parents to tell them hard things. Days that I've called my big brother through tears to ask him to pray. Mornings I've needed my mom more than before. These are days that make me feel as small as purple yarn in my pigtails and unicorns on my sneakers. Very small. Littlest sister small.

AT THIRTY-SEVEN, I am just beginning to learn that I am both grown, and still growing.

I'm learning that growing up is frantic calls to my dad when fat, green caterpillars show up on my tomato plants. It is also wondering if he is drinking enough water when the temperature soars to 85 degrees. Growing up is finding myself choosing not to be too busy, and happily driving two hours just to linger long over lunch with my mom. Being their daughter and the mother of my own gives me the capacity to know both as a gift. Seeing my parents as people was perhaps the greatest bequest that growing up afforded. Standing side by side with my brothers as we all steadily grow up is the next chapter of the Blythe kids—except now we have the added sobriety of knowing that though life is long, time is incredibly short.

THERE IS a richness to being this age and standing in this middle place that I never knew was coming. To stand firmly between small and grown and still feel both quite keenly. I want to cling, to grasp with white knuckles and gritted teeth to this time right now—quick, before anyone gets any older, from my daughters to their grandparents and everyone in between.

No matter how much time we have, we will always want more.

EVEN AS WE say goodbye at the end of a family dinner, a weekend, an afternoon, we never take any of it for granted.

We take what we are given and give thanks again. When our sides ache from laughter and the plates are scraped clean, we hug goodbye like liturgy—*and also with you.* We part amongst murmurs of "be careful, see you soon," which may as well be translated, "I love you even though you made fun of my kale salad."

· · ·

WHETHER OUR FAMILIES are so large that we eat on paper plates at Christmas, or much smaller and quieter—we see the gift. And in all its imperfect glory, it points upward.

This gift of family further illustrates its Giver, in vivid color. It comforts us to know that from one generation to the next, God is still at work to draw us closer to Himself and to one another.

We are all being held quite close by the sovereign One who has more authority than the ticking clock, the yearly physical, and the days that we cannot get back.

That fact alone comforts this grown up little girl.

REMEMBERING His sovereign care over me and the ones I love, I think perhaps I can manage to be this person. The one who worries about her in-laws and also smiles to see flecks of silver popping up around the temples of her own lifelong love. The one who wants to go back as much as she wants to smile at the future.

I can be her.

The girl who clasps both the certainty and the mystery of life in the middle—and receives them each with expectancy.

I count the grateful days and I slowly learn that I can be the mother of daughters and my parents' daughter, all at once. This middle place is not one without concern or fear, but a place marked by the merciful gift of composite perspective and hope.

For now, in this middle place of much grace— that will be enough.

KALE CAESAR SALAD WITH LEMON DRESSING

T he first time I tasted Kale Caesar Salad, all future Caesar Salads made with other, inferior greens were immediately sworn off.

There is something so lovely about crisp, sturdy kale that can stand up to a heavier dressing like Caesar. The most important thing to remember when making a Kale Salad is to massage the kale. It may sound wacky but it is the best four minutes you will spend and your reward will be a much better salad!

AND IF TIME isn't on your side and the Ten-Minute Croutons take ten minutes too long, toss a handful of broken pita chips in there and call it a day.

The crunch is our main concern, anyway. However if you happen to have ten extra minutes and half of a day- old baguette, the croutons are the worth the extra effort.

❧

PROVISIONS.

5 cups of raw, de-stemmed Kale

1/2 cup of grated parmesan cheese

1 lemon, zested and divided, (use half for the dressing.)

One shallot, sliced thinly and then sautéed in olive oil. Drain on paper towels and salt.

LEMON CAESAR DRESSING.

1/2 cup of Grated parmesan cheese

1/2 cup of Plain greek yogurt

3 tbs. Fresh lemon juice

1 1/2 tbs. Olive oil

1 tsp. Dijon mustard

2 tsp. Worcestershire sauce

1 Clove of garlic, minced

1 tsp. Anchovy paste

1/4 tsp. Kosher salt

Several grinds of cracked black pepper

2-3 tbs. Milk

Half of the lemon zest

.   .   .

METHOD. Remove large stems from kale and then tear into smaller pieces. Add to a large bowl and add half the lemon zest. Set aside.

Mix all ingredients of the dressing together except the milk. Add the milk gradually to your own desired consistency. A thicker dressing adheres better to the kale.

Set a timer for 4 minutes. Add 1 tbs. of dressing to the kale and then massage it in with your hands for 4 minutes. This softens the kale and removes the bitterness. The green color will deepen and your amount of kale will shrink dramatically.

Add parmesan, shallot, and about 1/2 cup of dressing to the kale and then toss well. Add more if needed. Top with Ten Minute Croutons.

TEN MINUTE CROUTONS

I am convinced that one of the main game-changers in a salad is the crunch. There are many ways to make a spectacular salad but a salad without some sort of crunch can be sort of sad.

These stovetop croutons are the perfect crunchy topping to the Kale Caesar Salad. You may use any rustic loaf of bakery or homemade bread. It should be crusty, but day old bread works beautifully for croutons. I have used multi-grain, french baguette, or rosemary parmesan loaves from Costco.

The point is less about the variety of bread, and more about the extra flavor and texture they add.

PROVISIONS.
    One Loaf of Rustic bread, cut into large cubes.
    Extra Virgin Olive Oil
    Italian Seasoning
    Parmesan Cheese
    Kosher Salt
    Cracked Pepper

A squeeze of lemon juice to finish

BEGIN.

Prepare a dry skillet to a medium hight heat. Toss the bread cubes in a large bowl with several tablespoons of olive oil, the Italian seasoning and salt and pepper. (You don't want the bread to be so oiled that it's soggy, just coated.)

Stir gently with a wooden spoon until the cubes have dried and become crispy and light brown on all sides. Top with parmesan and a very small squeeze of fresh lemon juice.

Taste for salt and pepper and add more if needed. Let cool slightly or serve warm on top of big bowl of green goodness.

Croutons will keep in a sealed container for 2-3 days.

5

A HOLLOW FULL OF HOPE

It is 2006 and at twenty-three, the roll of actual film I took this week holds moments worth keeping. Under a pink sunset at the beach, I meet my friend Lauren's new boyfriend (who later became her husband.) I sing loudly while another kindred, Heidi, blows out candles on a Publix cake with butter-cream icing and streamers made of frosting.

This is my spring break and I am visiting my first home, my whole huge family, and my Florida people.

Facebook is brand new. I only use my cell phone for calls, and email for long-distance conversations. Between school and work, my little circle of friends has lots of catching up to do.

We reunite over the life we have missed; even a stroll through Target is a glittery gift. Next to the post-it notes and pencils, one conversation turns into doubled-over laughter as we try not to wet our pants. It feels good to laugh with these people who know me well and know that my year has been the absolute pits.

Hours later, it is past eleven when I tiptoe in to see my parents on the couch; the television murmurs with an old sci-fi movie and they look up.

I have kept them up late and I feel a twinge of guilt, but they show only sleepy smiles. They are the best kind of parents who are always happy to see us happy; the kind who wait for us kids to arrive and then send us away with arms of leftovers, waving until our cars are down the street and out of sight.

I AM HALFWAY THROUGH COLLEGE. This year has been the hardest to date, a bleak winter of leaving behind things I truly thought I needed, things I thought I wanted. My fingers are sore from having these weights wrenched from my grasp, but now suddenly there is room to hold something better. For the first time, the absence holds space of a promise.

It feels like hope.

This week in my parents' house is the road sign of a new beginning. The smell of the grass and its dew blanket ministers to me. The clink of the coffee pot and the rub of my socks on their kitchen floor are all I need each morning to be glad I came.

Everything is fresh.

I'm tender but hopeful, like soft black soil mounded up, ready to hold and grow something new.

One afternoon, my Dad digs a deep hole in the front yard for a Meyer lemon tree. My brother and my nephew, Ben, lower the new plant into the hole. Ben grins from beneath his own garden hat, his five-year-old knees sticking out of black rubber boots.

Now in the ground, the lemon tree is two feet tall.

A FEW DAYS LATER, I hug my parents twice and back out of the driveway to return to school. The rocks scatter under my tires as I throw a hopeful glance in the direction of the tiny tree. Hope for growth and health. Hope for change for me and for it.

Hope seems to be all I have at the moment—but at the moment, it's exactly enough.

As I cross state lines and pass IHOP restaurants and gas stations, I can feel it. Those darker days are already beginning to fade.

After eight hours of driving and two stops, my apartment is cool and smells like comfort and unlit Yankee candles. Pajamas found, I slide my unpacked suitcase over and climb into bed. Somehow the rock in my chest seems smaller, softer. The pain isn't gone but it is shrinking—leaving a hopeful space, a welcome emptiness behind.

THIRTEEN YEARS HAVE PASSED since that sunny spring and I have not forgotten the darker parts of the story, though they are a watery blend of events. Sifting through for the express purpose of remembering, I can still feel the rough upholstery of the couch under my fingertips, the one I sat on for two days straight. I remember the months of looking over my shoulder, willing my phone not to ring. But more than all of this, I recall that night in my own twin-sized bed. The night I realized the gray inside me had begun to shade into another, lighter color.

Now when my tires spin those same rocks, it is no longer just me and my one little bag on the front seat. The car is packed to the edges with my blue-eyed love and two little people who look like us both, plus a large, happy dog. It is a car full of the epilogue to that one particular story. It is not that I don't remember, or that I am merely strong and resilient.

My life is not so marked by bravery or bliss that I cannot be touched by a sickening remembrance.

HOWEVER.

It was a side road. Nothing more. The kind of wrong turn you don't mean to take that leads to somewhere you did not mean to go. Once you realize that where you are is not where you should be, you do your best to get the heck out of there and get back on the main road. If you have ever taken a wrong turn that needed to end with a U-turn, then you know. It matters less that people see you turn around; it matters more that you are headed in the right direction. Of little consequence, that you veered off course; of chief importance, that you were saved from ending up at the wrong destination.

My ONCE TINY nephew is now much taller than me. The lemon tree towers over him. In late November, the branches weigh heavy with bright yellow fruit. Between stirring cranberry sauce and baking pumpkin pie, we run outside my parents' house to pick armfuls of lemons, some to enjoy right away and a few to carry gently home to our blue house.

Each year I stand under this tree and I am grateful. Not just because that season eventually faded, but because no part of it was wasted. Because my Maker used it to make something brand new in me. I rejoice, not as a result of a happy ending, but of a realization that I was never alone.

OUR DEEPEST PAIN often digs the well of a deep hollow place. A kind of rooting out naturally takes place when we hurt. Thank goodness we aren't responsible for the rooting itself. No, we are too busy taking breaths, getting out of bed, doing the next thing — even if the next thing is remembering to buy food and eat dinner. This hollow place that pain creates— it is a place that can be completely cleansed of all we didn't know we needed to lose.

. . .

THERE WAS SO MUCH I did not know about my God before I experienced deep pain. So much experiential faith that I needed for my future. There are things we need to offload in order to be whole, parts of ourselves that we might not have willingly released if we hadn't been recovering from the whiplash of sorrow.

Now I find myself grateful for it all.

Grateful even for greater times of sorrow I have walked since then. Eventually, deeper times of grief and loss came that I could not chalk up to being a bad judge of character. Times when I felt my fingers stretch open again as things my heart desperately wanted slipped away on the wind.

Strangely, these fresher times of loss without someone to blame removed the sting of what was before. What seemed so weighty is light and inconsequential when heavier pain comes along.

Those days all those years ago—days of sacred rescue that at the time felt like sheer abandonment? They are altogether faded. Hindsight produced a glimpse that grew into forbearance for what others have walked.

I have been forgiven much. Christ in me forgives and forgives again every time I remember.

WHEN NEW GRIEF rolls us over with its undertow, we need something to hold on to. We need stones of remembrance. Just as we cannot rush the ripening of fruit, the process of healing cannot be hurried.

We lose parents, lose jobs, lose babies, lose friends, lose our way, and we forget who we are in the pain. In places that only held comfort and a place for us, we find we no longer belong and we forget who we belong to.

Our first newborn cries echo into an already broken world. Arriving brand new, we already bear the scars of a curse we cannot escape. We are a people who will never feel completely at rest, completely at home, and solely without pain or grief. A people on their way home are never at rest until they arrive.

And we are not home yet.

And in the meantime? We live in the in-between.

The pain God lovingly allows I want to greet as a gift. Not because I relish it and I definitely do not in the moment, but as He heals something in me that desperately needs healing, I grow more aware of my weakness. In the in-between, we can want the ache to end and yet still know He is good.

SOMEONE ONCE SAID that time does not heal, but God does. I agree in part. True, every single shred of healing we have comes straight from the Great Physician who carved our hearts with His hands. But He also gave us the gift of time.

Time is a gift wrapped in an unknown number of days and tied with the ribbon that what comes next will be even better.

Time is what we have now, I believe one of the reasons He gives it to us is for healing—not that we would be more comfortable, but that we would be more able to reflect who He is.

So yes, time does heal; but only because God uses it to heal something in us.

In the in-between, there is no other option but to keep my chin lifted towards the light and the truth.

Hope is a lifeline. But hope itself, as a word, as a noun, has very little power. I can emblazon the word on a sweatshirt and wear it all year, but it is not a talisman against pain. Hope is full of all that we cannot yet see—and all that we can see when we look back from where we are. But truly, the only power hope has ever had is that Hope is a person. All our longings and emptiness are filled with our Hope. Because He came to us—Immanuel—but also because He stays with us.

. . .

THERE ARE moments when in negligence I forget to remember all that He has done to give me Himself, to be my redemption, my hope, and my inheritance. Countless moments that my hope feels hollow and without a way in or out. In those moments, it is my one job to remember. To remember what He has already said and done.

WHEN GRIEF COMES, as it surely will, we look up. We look back at how many battles He has already fought for us, and we keep our chins pointed up. Dear friend, when we have nothing else, we have Him and the truth of His word—the knowledge that He will never leave us.

EVERY YEAR, the lemons ripen in their own sweet and slightly tart time. We pick them faithfully and enjoy them for months. We use them to flavor our water, we squeeze them over salads, we bake them into scones.

With every flake of zest that scatters lemony mist into the air and every drop of sunny juice, I remember the beginning of that particular tree, the stalky little bunch of sticks. I recall the girl who stood next to it and wondered how God would possibly redeem the mess in her lap.

He did weave my mess into something new. But all along, when the new was still on the way, I was never alone.

Every time I stretch up and pick a shiny lemon, I remember that even when I hurt, He is always, always good. When we cannot see how something new will fill a place hollowed by pain, His goodness is there growing something remarkable.

And sometimes, a hollow full of hurt is simply a newly emptied space ready to hold something beautiful.

MEYER LEMON SCONES

P uffy lemon scones with texture and a tart glaze are the
spring breakfast treat of my dreams. They pair beautifully
with black coffee & scrambled eggs in the morning, Iced Coffee
in the afternoon, and just about any time in between.

If Meyer Lemons are out of season, or cost as much as a
Disney Cruise, substitute regular lemons or even navel oranges.
Either way, they will be citrusy and glorious!

PROVISIONS.
2 cups of All-Purpose Flour

1/3 cup Raw sugar
1 tbs. Baking Powder
1/2 tsp. Kosher salt
zest of two lemons
1 1/2 cups heavy cream

GLAZE.
1 cup of Powdered Sugar
The juice of one lemon, tbsp. Lemon zest
Mix until thick and glossy but able to be drizzled

METHOD. (By Hand.)
Preheat oven to 425'F
In a medium bowl, add all dry ingredients and whisk. Add zest
Mix in the cream and stir gently until combined into a loose, wet ball.
Turn out on a floured surface. Pat into a circle and then cut into wedges.

BAKE ON A PARCHMENT paper lined baking sheet for 12-14 minutes until puffy and lightly golden brown.
Cool completely before topping with lemon glaze.

6

THREE GALLONS OF MILK & THE SOVEREIGNTY OF GOD

L ate afternoon light slants through the kitchen window, splashing a checkerboard on the table, the floor, and everything in its path. At the kitchen counter, I chop sweet potatoes to roast for dinner and see a car pulling into the driveway. I glance at the time. Three o'clock. It cannot be Lance home from work yet.

But it is.

I meet him on our small side porch.

He holds a box of things all jumbled together. Sinking, I piece together the time of day, the slight slump of his shoulders, and the contents of the box peeking above the cardboard edge. Our eyes meet and I know that the thing we have feared for over a year has finally come to awful fruition. Where yesterday Lance had a "good enough for right now" job at a local university, he suddenly holds only free time and the sting of being unceremoniously axed. Because of endless restructuring, he was not so politely let go.

We hug long and my arms cannot squeeze hard enough to make amends for the way he has been treated recently. Our four-year-old and 18-month-old girls come running to the familiar creak of the kitchen door. Turning our faces to them, we artificially mirror their broad smiles.

Moments later they return to a pile of princess Little People figures and we hide in the pantry/ laundry room. My frantic, whispered questions are muffled by a lone pair of jeans dancing around the dryer drum.

There are no answers, really. Just questions. My always calm husband is deflated but still calm; I am as irate as a she-bear at the close of winter. Even as we agree it is all for the best, my internal dialogue is shrill and tuned to panic.

How could they?

THE NEXT MORNING AT BREAKFAST, no one is in a rush to throw down eggs before the clock strikes. No lunches are packed and we plan to visit the park as a family. We make lemonade out of the lemons we've been given and revel in our sudden bittersweet gift of time. I make two iced coffees during nap time and Lance joins me in my daily rhythm of reset accompanied by caffeine.

The days that follow are a jumble of questions and nuance, punctuated by moments of normalcy.

I realize we are out of milk and grab my keys while he sits at the kitchen table to research the many red-taped details of the state of being unemployed. There may be a specialized government website for the jobless, but the process is more tangled than the earbuds at the bottom of my purse.

STEPPING toward the dairy aisle at Publix, the knowledge hits me.

We are a four-person family with a zero dollars a year plus nothing salary.

If you have ever been in this place, then you know how scary it can be. You should be rational and remember that this is America and of course there are jobs out there for people who want them. You should note all the truths you know, but instead you picture the faces of your children and have irrational fears of them going without. Instead of knowing very well and trusting that we would be just fine, my heart broke open at the thought of running out of milk and not being able to refill my girls' cups. What I knew to be true temporarily faded in favor of what was right in front of my face.

So I did what any partially sane mother would do—I marched straight to the milk and put three gallons in my cart instead of the usual one. There, I thought. Now we are okay for almost three weeks. As if having three gallons of milk would make us okay, when internally, we were far from it.

In that moment, there was nothing wrong with buying extra milk. But when I came through the door and had to explain to Lance why I basically procured a cow, I knew I was wrong. Instead of resting in what I knew to be true, I was coping. Instead of taking time to sit in the grief of the loss and uncertainty, I got up too quickly and took my own stoic precautions. I hurt for myself and I hurt for him and I didn't know how to say it loud enough. Instead of searching for the words, I did load after load of laundry and made pots of soup and mentally chose which boxes I would pack first when we inevitably had to move again. I located the packing tape and began to quietly tidy junk drawers thinking we would have to dump them into empty Amazon boxes before the month ended. I cried in the shower so that my dear, hurting husband wouldn't know how much his own hurt caused searing pain within me. It may have all been normal, but it wasn't all helpful. Stoicism and resilience were my tools of battle instead of trust and rest; stiff, silent bravery rather than quiet acceptance and praise.

. . .

WE LEARNED MUCH in this stage of being suddenly unemployed. We learned that the extensive process for stating that you are in need of a job makes it complicated to actually find said job. The two of us together gained a great deal of compassion for others in the same predicament and we lost all our pious under-standing once we recognized how ignorant we were of job-related struggles.

I also learned that I am far more equipped to endure pain myself than to observe someone I love being wronged. For Lance and me, this situation was more than a personnel deci-sion. The way it was handled, it was a blatant disregard for his person altogether. He was injured yet took it in humility while I was left gaping at their gall and hoping not to run into his former boss at the grocery store.

There are few things more injurious to the human heart than standing by while someone you love deeply suffers deeply. I will not say it hurt more than when we lost a baby—because one is one and one is another. But I will say it was the same kind of visceral, sudden pain that made me want to stand on a chair with a megaphone and shout my cries of injustice.

If you have stood in that place of wanting to deflect pain and absorb it yourself, then you know. You know that there is a rare sweetness in suffering together. In loving someone so much and feeling such injustice at how the world, or even a tiny, insignificant corner of the world, views that person that it physically hurts to take a breath. This is what it means to be one flesh and to share in pain so deeply that you, for a moment, forget everything else.

You may even forget that suffering together is just as much a part of marriage as those incandescent moments of joy shared and doubled. In reality, the ache has as much potential to further sew us to one another as the moments in which we laugh and hug, resplendent, as happiness squeezes from our eyes. All the moments that make a marriage make it full and true. Never have I felt more like my husband's partner than when we were huddled together shielding our family from what felt like an all-out air raid.

In spite of the fact that I now recall that season with warmth and a smile, it did not feel like a kindness at the time. It felt cruel and unusual, like getting a speeding ticket on the way to the funeral of someone you love.

Still.

I would change nothing about that brief but shaky time except my reaction to it and the handful of mistakes I wish I could undo.

The first mistake was of course that I bought three gallons of milk with the same expiration date. (We made a lot of pudding.)

Second, I held bitterness toward people I did not actually know. Bitterness dries up the parts of us that hold warmth and understanding and leaves us feeling worse than we thought we could. Bitterness costs valuable energy. When we are in the midst of a maelstrom-like season, we simply do not have energy to spend on the poor choices of someone else. Harboring anger may seem to poke the smoldering logs and embolden our hearts, but really it reduces us to dry ash and crowds out the voice of God.

Perhaps my greatest mistake was that I forgot the sovereignty of God. I forgot that God is always good, even when good people make bad decisions and bang up everyone in their calamitous path.

What we know to be true is that the sovereignty of God is not an abstract idea. It is not a hypothetical wish that we hang all our expectations on while reading Him a list in prayer form of exactly what we think we need. God's sovereignty is neither a side note nor an embellishment to pull out when things go pear-shaped. It is an understanding—a knowledge that goes all the way down—that none of this surprised Him in the slightest.

Sovereignty points directly to the concept of authority, and God's authority over all that we endure means that He is worthy of our trust. Sovereignty means He is not scrambling or throwing together a plan when we are knee deep in disbelief over what has landed in our laps today. He is already there, hemming us in on every side.

WE MAY BE familiar with Romans 8:28, words that embolden our hearts that "God works all things for the good of all who love Him." And perhaps we have tripped over this promise in the past when we cannot see any fragment of good that could come from a searingly awful situation.

In our uncertainty, we want to grasp the promise that it will all turn out okay in the end—which is absolutely true, if you and I can agree on what "the end" means, if we can agree that the end we speak of is much closer to being a beginning. Still, in our pain and fog and seasons of pure, unadulterated blah, we may forget that what is for our good will rarely feel good when we are walking through it.

EVEN AS WE wait on Him to renew our strength, we walk on. This season that Lance and I endured reminded me that the manner in which we walk matters so much more than the distance we cover. For the first few weeks after the bottom fell out, my survival instincts were to avoid everyone but the people in our blue house, to pull in our sidewalks and live one day at a time. As we walk through cyclical seasons of hurt, avoidance can feel like a survival skill. We may be tempted to adopt an "us against the world" perspective, especially when it feels safer to trust no one while we reel in pain. Keeping to ourselves while we deal with emotions we do not want feels like the best option. Emotional hibernation, though necessary for a short season, should not be where we stay.

But God.

He came to us through the mercy of every unconventional place you don't always expect to meet Him.

At a routine visit to the doctor, a wrinkled strip of paper taped to the back of the receptionist's computer reminded me in Comic Sans 12, "The Lord will fight for you, you need only to be still." (Exodus 14:14 NIV)

In the preschool pickup line, a note came through my window that an anonymous friend paid Lucy's monthly tuition. I pulled over to let grateful tears fall as her four-year-old voice rose up from the back seat with a song I didn't know she knew. "Oh how He loves you and me . . . . Oh how He loves you and me . . . ." In that sacred moment in a church parking lot, I could not have felt more seen. By the mysterious friend, and by the God who both prompted them and my tiny serenade from the back seat.

Day after day the mailbox held brightly colored cards stuck in amongst water bills and advertisements. Every one a reminder of His faithfulness in the scrawled handwriting of friends.

Our God was a kind companion when we were mashed up and wounded, to show us we were not alone, not forgotten, and not floundering nearly as much as we felt.

We would all like to believe Fraulein Maria and the Reverend Mother that whenever God closes a door, somewhere He begins opening a window. But it is the in-between time that stings our core and drives us to distraction. We stand stunned in a hallway, still hearing the echo of a door that slammed in our faces in such a profound and un-openable way. A breathless wait ensues—until the window is visible, the drapes are joyfully thrown aside, and the latch is loosened to reveal fresh cool air and a clear path.

For our family, our window came just weeks later. The next direction was a gift in every possible way and most of the things that we feared never even came close to our doorstep.

But even if they had, what we knew to be true proved more powerful than the fog in front of us or a path directly through it. What was true on that September day will be true in every abruptly cloudy season you and I face in the following days.

The sovereignty of God will always be worth more than our frantic preparations to shield those that we love from what we cannot avoid.

What we know to be true is worth far more than having a false sense of provision.

It is worth more than having three gallons of milk in the refrigerator.

It is worth the open-handed acceptance that He is a good Father and He does all things well.

CHARCUTERIE & THE AT-HOME DATE NIGHT

Early on in our life as parents, Lance and I realized how crazy expensive it could be to go on a date and pay for a babysitter too. Occasionally we would take the plunge and shell out for a sweet teenage girl to tuck our children in while we ate dinner out, but more often than not— we had the need to connect far more often than the budget would allow. Enter the at-home date night. Once a week, usually on a weekend, we feed the girls early, put them to bed and then run downstairs to have a separate dinner by ourselves.

A star player in our at-home date nights still is, the charcuterie board. It's fast, can be completely prepped ahead of time, and can be eaten on the living room floor by two exhausted parents who want to clink their glasses of LaCroix together and then watch a movie while eating their grown up cheese and crackers.

Charcuterie is textbook *Feasting & Foraging*. It is the ideal poster child for odds and ends making a meal. Bringing cheeses, meats, fruit and crackers together adds up to be so much more than that glorified lunchable that we grew up wishing our moms would pack us, (really it was all about those two token Oreo cookies.)

To make a charcuterie board or platter— you may essentially use anything you want— but I try to follow this basic blueprint, by choosing 1-2 from each category if it is available. Play around with different cheeses and meats— but focus on having some variety of flavor, texture, and color. Sometimes, if we haven't had enough vegetables that day, I'll dress a small bit of greens with vinaigrette and add that right to the board. There really aren't that many rules— and any rules at all are loosey-goosey.

~

Building a Charcuterie Board

3-4 Cheeses
- Hard: Parmesan, Romano
- Semi-Hard: Apple-Smoked Gouda, or if you live near Trader Joe's, the Unexpected Cheddar is a favorite for us.
- Fragrant: Blue, Roquefort, Feta (marinated or not.)
- Soft: Boursin, Brie, Goat, (we often pair a favorite peach pepper jelly with Brie or Goat.)

Meats
- Peppered Salami

- Prosciutto
- Soppressata
- Bresaola
- Sausage
- Sliced Turkey or Chicken (it works!)

Fruits
- Crisp Red Grapes
- Thinly Sliced Tart Apple
- Dried Apricots
- Sliced Peaches in summer or a few Berries
- Clementine Segments

Spreads & Condiments
- Fig Jam
- Pepper Jelly
- Spicy Mustard
- Honey
- Chutney
- Tapenade

Extras & More
- Sliced Baguette
- Cheese Crisps
- Regular or Gluten Free Crackers
- Raw Sweet Pepper
- Roasted Nuts
- Marinated Olives
- Honeyed Almonds

One more note, do not fret if you don't have one of those beautiful weathered boards, any platter will work. I've even used a cookie sheet draped with a cute linen napkin— the more rustic, the better.

7

HOMESICKNESS & THE BLUE HOUSE

When our family first came to Georgia, we had only one child and mobile phones that slid open and shut. Our street was named after a golfer and held a cozy, two-bedroom patio home with a dishwasher and railroad tracks twenty feet from the back door.

We arrived Halloween weekend and, because of the economy of our new living space, unpacked in record time. We even slipped in a fall festival at a local church at the tail end of our first few days.

At 18 months old, Lucy surveyed her new kingdom and began an immediate reign of unpacking things that should be packed and taking apart things that should remain together. The move from North Carolina marked my first days as a stay-at-home mom and I was just happy to be there with her—unfazed by her creative destruction and as charmed by her chatter as I was with her footie pajamas.

As moving always requires, there was an adjustment period. We found the grocery store and the post office and the library with its rows of young maple trees.

While I still needed a GPS to run basic errands, our joy-bringer Lucy acclimated immediately with no reservations. Each time our front tires rolled into our one-car driveway, she yelled out, "Oh! My House!" with a wide grin.

Just after Christmas, we packed up again and moved into a gray house with a wide front porch and several scraggly, under-loved azalea bushes. It took Lucy only three days before her sing-song words floated from the backseat, "Our house!"

Two months later, our gray house officially became the Blue House when it was painted the perfect shade of Williamsburg blue. That same day after we went out, Lucy cheerfully chirped upon our return, "Oh! My Blue House!"

WHAT A HAPPY ACCEPTANCE for a toddler to have about living in two states and three different houses within one quarter of her little life.

She was thrilled to be there, just happy to be home—wherever home was.

I, however, took a little longer to be truly settled. More than a few months, in fact. Flowers bloomed, leaves colored and then danced down, turning our backyard into a variegated crunchy carpet. Seasons in the Blue House strung together in my heart like a string of café lights—draping our life with the knowledge that this was our home, even if home was still something we were breaking in.

BOXES WERE UNPACKED. Easter eggs were dyed, hidden, and found. Soon a Christmas tree stood sentry in the living room, followed by February which brought our bright-eyed baby Abby. By early summer, birthday parties were held the length of the front porch. From Friday nights with pizza and paper plates to Saturday mornings spent exploring a still new-to-us town, I found my heart inexplicably in two places at once. The oaks that encircled our house gave my heart a certain swell— but so did an unexpected sighting of someone else's North Carolina license plate. The longer we stayed, the more embarrassed I became of my heart's dichotomy. The deeper I tried to stretch roots where we were, the more it hurt to remember where we had been. I questioned why I couldn't just be happy with this job, this house, this life— all an answer to a long-whispered prayer.

Daily I wondered how long the journey of belonging would take.

AUTHOR CHRISTIE PURIFOY often refers to place-making and never has a word better explained my heart for home. Place-making articulates the desire that pulls within me. So strong is my belief that where we are matters, that I want the spaces I steward and cultivate to be spaces of true belonging.

IN ALL THIS focus on being a soft landing for those given to me to love, I often forget that with every new relationship, memory, and experience, my roots are going deeper. Perhaps this is why others seem so much stronger when they must say goodbye to places they love; I am the one who holds on after everyone else has let go; my roots go all the way down. Anne Shirley spoke for many of us when she said, "I've put out a lot of little roots these two years . . . and when I go they're going to hurt to pull up."

They do. They always do. But maybe it isn't such a bad thing after all.

.   .   .

IN EIGHT YEARS of having belonging placed in my hands and not always choosing to see it, I have often been too distracted to settle in. I wonder if maybe you have felt the split, too. The crazy feeling of being torn between two places you love, loving them both and not wanting to lose either one. The murkiness of being caught between a "not yet" and an "already," where both places feel both familiar and foreign to such a degree that you might as well just smile and cry for both.

If you have ever driven away to feel a lump in your throat for what lies in your rear view mirror, you are not alone.

Grief over a geographical location can be its own brand of happy homesickness; one that brings us to a place of understanding. It is the whispered reminder that we will never in our lives not feel a small ache for somewhere or something.

Slowly, I am learning that this reoccurring ache is a gift, not a curse.

FIVE YEARS after our last visit to North Carolina, we finally went back to our first home together. Just the two of us. The original Lance and Cindy—the duo who took late night walks and said "We will, forever" on a campus we loved. In the bitterest of the bittersweet, we went back to say goodbye to the friend who brought us together.

Dr. R. Logan Carson was a pastor, teacher, friend, and employer to both of us. In fact, we had our first real conversation facing each other with his kitchen island between us. He was a willing participant in our finding each other and so it was only right that he stood in that warm wooded chapel and led us in our vows. Dr. Carson was a dear friend to us both. At eighty-six years old, his race was over and he stepped through the door where no pain or horrors can follow.

For a brief forty-eight hours, we walked those brick paths

again. We said goodbye. Our feet crunched over a Wake Forest autumn and we dined on memories and tacos. And when it was over, we went home.

On the way back to our girls and Blue House, a rightness rose in me like a bright bubble. I noticed a very clear pivot, a directional shift—we did not spend the hours driving to reminisce or talk about what was behind us, but instead focused on what was ahead. Our car and our conversation both rightly pointed in the direction of home.

We raced back to sit side by side in a dimly lit room and watch our daughters perform in a play. Their faces shone as they smiled at us from the stage. They were most evidently in an element of comfort and belonging, and so were we. The fact that we were home was clear and comfortable, and there was no ache in my heart for where we had just been that morning.

SOMEWHERE IN THE past eight years—and much sooner than I realized—a shift occurred. Now I know that the sometimes constant ache was not homesickness at all, but the ripple effects of belonging somewhere and being changed by it. We were affected in a way that would not easily fade with a new driver's license and electric company.

The severing of one city of belonging and the stitching up of another in its place is meant to cause an ache. What a welcome ache it is, though, to know that we have loved and been shaped by a place so beautiful that it left an endearing mark upon us all.

Not the mark of a scar, but like the etches in a well-used table.

The lines that testify to the thousands of meals, one right after the other in rhythmic succession.

The imprints of a life lived in an ordinary place, a place that proves magical because of its end result. We made a place there, for ourselves and those we loved.

We lived there and left our mark—but the deepest mark was of that place on us. As we set about the business of making our place here, our darling former town slowly faded as the place we belonged—just as it should.

THOUGH WE DIG DEEPLY where we are and rightfully so, this boomerang nostalgia is still not one we should discount. Knowing that we are exactly where we need and want to be, we can still treasure the places we have been. The goal is to hold them close without idealizing or causing a deficit to our own places of belonging. We can love our former homes, jobs, churches, and communities without being discontent for where our feet are planted today.

And for me, that knowledge feels like sacred progress.

So often we cling to those locales that marked our lives when we are not meant to stay there. We were marked so that we may go out and scatter, making a continual and spreading mark like concentric ripples on a lake with the hope that is in us.

WHEREVER WE ARE PLANTED IS where we will truly belong—even if it feels foreign, even if it is only for a season. Here, today, is where I should be. With my house and its thin windows that whisper wind in the winter months. Here with my backyard and its wooden fence and wild felicity of trees. Here is home.

And for our family, it matters less if we live here, in this house, forever, or find ourselves driving a For Sale sign into soft earth sometime before our girls leave elementary school. As much as this Blue House endears itself to me with every passing season, I guard against clinging too tightly to a place that may not always be mine.

PERHAPS THE ACHE of a home that is no longer yours is much better than never feeling that pull of restlessness. Restlessness can be a gift when it reminds us that we are not actually going to be at home anywhere in this life. In the first book of the Wingfeather Saga, Andrew Peterson calls homesickness "a joy that hurts."

It is a joy to belong, and it does hurt.

If you have learned to live with the throb of homesickness and belonging, take heart. Know that the small, lingering ache of home in the corner of your heart is not an ache that should or ever will be satisfied. You and I carry the ache within us, to long for something familiar, beautiful, and formative.

Whether it hurts a little or so much that you take only shallow breaths for a time, know that the ache is there to illustrate something priceless. We are headed home and we are not there yet.

IN THE MEANTIME, however long our time gift happens to be, gratefulness changes our vision. The daily reaching for thanks when we might feel inclined to see what we lack—these are the lenses we need. If I am not looking up, I will miss the way the trees stretch bare to a January sky, fragmenting the blue sky into a million tiny puzzle pieces.

MAY both the thrill and the ache of what we know cause us to keep looking up, savoring our gift of time, trusting where we have been planted, and spending well the days we have.

When the staggering ache causes us to we feel that we don't

truly belong anywhere at all, still may we keep looking up. Change can be bitterly hard, but we are a people of hope. A people who are given the promise that we are never, ever alone —regardless of how the landscape out our kitchen window may change.

When I forget to remember that I am here for a purpose that is not my own, I need the recollection that gratefulness brings. I want to pay better attention to the details of my days that whisper of God's sovereignty and kind mercy to me.

I want to wear these lenses of hope and never take them off. The lenses that cause my eyes to chase the light.

To see the beauty in both the backyard bathed in slanting afternoon light and the once-in-a-lifetime trip with suitcase full and passport stamped. To pay full-faced attention to the lilting sounds of my daughters' laughter as though I have never heard it before. I want mine to be eyes that look for the lovely and when I see it all around me, I want it to lift my gaze, up, up, up to the Giver of both the gift and these eyes with which to see it.

All around, there is evidence of how loved we are; may we not miss the beauty that is unapologetically lifting our chins up in thanks.

WHETHER WE ARE SETTLED with roots that go all the way down or still trying to determine where the couch looks best, our places and the lives we make in them—they are all for His purpose and glory.

Sometimes we find home all at once, and other times we have to let it happen gradually, painfully, naturally—both are a gift in the making.

And in the meantime, we will choose not to force it. We will not chide ourselves into feeling settled.

We will choose instead, the really good pizza and a porch

picnic and the mingled scent of citronella and pepperoni on the first warm night of spring.

We will choose touring our own town, old or new, on a Saturday morning or Monday night.

We will not wait to begin making an imprint where we are, even when we feel odd and out of place.

We will begin loving where we are, here and now—and know that today, we are at least a little bit— home.

MAPLE SPICED PECANS

These pecans are infinitely better than store bought and they take mere minutes to pull together. Use them to dress up a salad, yogurt parfait, ice cream, or even a bowl of butternut squash soup.

They are a fall favorite in the BlueHouse.

PROVISIONS.

2 tbsp salted butter
2 tbsp maple syrup
2 tbsp brown sugar
2 cups pecan halves
1/8 tsp. Allspice
1/8 tsp. Cinnamon

METHOD.

Preheat oven to 350'F. Line a cookie sheet with parchment paper.

Melt butter in a saucepan over medium heat.

Add sugar and maple syrup and stir mixture until it begins to bubble.

Turn off the heat, add the allspice and stir.

Stir in the pecans and coat them well.

Spread pecans out on the parchment lined cookie sheet and then bake for 7-8 minutes.

Cool.

HARVEST SALAD WITH CIDER VINAIGRETTE

Provisions.
    4 cups of mixed spring greens
2 apples, thinly sliced
Dried cherries
Maple Spiced Pecans
2 roasted chicken breasts, thinly sliced (I use a rotisserie chicken.)

CIDER VINAIGRETTE.
    1/4 cup apple cider vinegar
1/2 tsp dijon mustard
3/4 tsp allspice
1/4 tsp cinnamon
1/4 kosher salt
1/4 tsp black pepper
1/2 cup + 2 tbsp extra virgin olive oil

. . .

METHOD. Mix all dressing ingredients except oil in a jar with tight fitting lid. Shake to incorporate. Drizzle oil in and shake again. Set aside.

Top greens with apple slices, cherries, roasted chicken, and pecans.

Shake dressing once more and drizzle on top.

Top with fresh ground pepper. Feel free to add a bit of crumbled goat cheese, though it doesn't actually need it.

I like to serve this salad with multigrain bread, soft salted butter, and a cold Pellegrino.

8

LIGHT THE CANDLES

"Happiness can be found in the darkest of times, if one only remembers to turn on the light." —Albus Dumbledore

L ate in November, we light candles on an ordinary Sunday night and there it is—hope—sneaking into our weary places.

THE CANDLES BEGIN to glow and drip in the middle of an ordinary supper. Outside is a drizzly soup of gray, wet, and cold and if you press your fingertips to the single-paned windows, you can feel just how far away spring is. The sky above is larger this time of year as the trees have all surrendered their leaves, making both the clear and gloomy days go on and on. Lighting candles around a simple meal feels extravagant, but we do it anyway.

We are the usual four plus my mom, who is visiting as she often does in the fall. When I was away at college, she began to visit each October. Some years we took a short trip together, Williamsburg or Asheville—other years we simply soaked up the glory of autumn in Wake Forest, together. Years later, we both know what a consolation it is to sip lattes and step on crunchy, colorful leaves shoulder to shoulder. It now feels like a mandate that we see each other between Halloween and Christmas.

But tonight, we both hold heavy hearts that waver between gifts and griefs.

We have this beautiful life resplendent with blessing—yet we also shoulder the burden of dear friends in another state who stand vigil over an isolette that holds their baby son and his broken heart. The outcome is still very much unknown and the updates are brief and sudden, sandwiched between hours of silence.

I feel helpless and anxious and my hope flickers like the ghostly glow of a dying light bulb. There is nothing I can do but intercede for them, for the doctors, for that small wonder of a boy.

So I roast a chicken.

I stand sentinel at my kitchen counter and cut thick slices of carrot and onion and baste every 15 minutes. And I light the tall candles like it is my job—I light them for the warm glowing reminder that hope is always better than despair. Hope is an act that becomes muscle memory when life is bleak or steeped in mundanity. It is the best kind of obstinance—this choosing to reach for the matches.

In this electricity-laden culture, candles can be something of a luxury to us. What once brought the only light after the sun went down, is now an extra, a bonus, a thing we must remember to do on purpose. All through the warmth of summer, these candles lie in a drawer and keep company with linen napkins. Almost forgotten in July, they are like oxygen to us in the dreariness of a very wet autumn.

But then, light is sacred to us when we remember our desperate need for it, isn't it?

PLATES FILLED, chairs occupied, forks and knives reflecting the glint of glowing candles. We hold hands in a circle around the table and say grace, a whispered prayer that feels like thank you, thank you, and please, please, God—be near. Be near to us both in these gifts we do not deserve and in fear we cannot muscle into words. Be near to us as our joy bubbles over again and comes in waves right alongside all that we struggle under. Be near to our friends who are to us like kindred.

THE WEIGHT of waiting is heavy and we linger longer than normal. Through dinner to the last bites of dessert, as the girls scatter to find cozy pajamas and beloved stuffed friends, running back in for one more hug and knock-knock joke.

And no joy feels truer here than the joy mashed up right against fear and uncertainty. We know it isn't ever "either or," but always "both and." Our hope has branches that always seem to carry the weight of heavier things. We hold hope and fear with our two hands and both are equally ponderous.

The phone on the counter buzzes with an update, asking for prayer—right then, that very second—needing intercession. We know what weary sounds like when their news is the worst possible kind. We know the dichotomy of holding hope and fear as we hold both with them. We know love and loyalty when we ache as those we care for ache. Struggling to taste the pie on our plates with the sudden rock in our throats, it is the lump we cannot swallow away.

As the candle glow bounces in the silence, we pray again.

. . .

LATER THE PLATES are all cleared and the dishwasher sings its soapy background song as a nine-year-old sneaks down the stairs past bedtime to show another lost tooth. She is all pink cheeks, pink pajamas, glittering eyes, and quiet giggles, clicking her tongue back and forth in the sudden void.

And it never gets old to her, nor to me. This thing, this tiny thing to happen on a Sunday night is the thing that brings us back to now. Smiles and lost teeth late at night muddle together with the knowledge that those we love are suffering and scared.

She runs back up the stairs, Ziploc bag in hand, containing her small white baby tooth.

My face cracks as she softly closes her bedroom door, because it seems that smiles and fear should not occupy the same ninety seconds in our living room. We celebrate a visit from the Tooth Fairy while we breathe frantic prayers for our friends who sit in a hospital room. And I want the assurance that our prayers will be answered in an extravagant way, I want to know that this little lion-hearted boy we pray for will one day smile at his parents through his own gaping grin.

But there are no answers. Not yet. Only the lavish assurance that as we pray to the God who sees even as we drift off to sleep, He guards all things well.

IN THE MORNING I meet my mom in the sun-splashed kitchen as Lance pours cups of coffee. Sometime before dawn, we received a quick message, a few words to let us know he made it through the procedure, through the night, through the first of many hurdles.

And it may not seem like much, but this and the sun unabashedly pouring through the windows are enough. A welcome harbinger of what is to come.

. . .

I TRULY BELIEVE that there is always cause for unhindered hope, that there is nothing we lose in the act of hoping. As image bearers of Christ, this hope that is graven on our hearts is not free from anguish, it is not exempt from the possible weight of the opposite outcome. Many of us have stood there, in that place not of abundance, but of scarcity. A place where we held in our hands the uncoiled end of an unhappy ending. And it hurts.

There are still corners of my heart, deep in the back, where the answer to my prayers stung deeply. Places where my hope took a beating and is still wounded.

I do not write about hope because it is easy for me; I write about hope because it is not.

But I know this like I know a good doughnut deserves hot, black coffee—hope is worth every bit of the fight.

AS WE LIFT up our eyes to the source of our hope, we know it is strong enough to carry both these weighty prayers and the knowledge that we may not get the outcome we cry out for.

This hope and the God who gives it to us can take it, because He came to us—to dwell among us while we were still dragged down by the curse. The snaking vines of brokenness that ran inside our DNA from the moment we lay squalling in the newborn nursery do not exempt us from our need—they are the reason for it. We were in need then and we are in need now. All these griefs that lay right alongside gifts, they are a mercy as they edge us closer to His side. Closer to the knowledge that we are nothing if not in need.

SINCE THAT NIGHT in November there have been both foggier and brighter days, both outside my kitchen window and for the ones I care deeply for.

At some point the following summer, this friend and I and all our children somehow had the rare gift of a single beach day together. We stood on the shore of the Atlantic, handing out watermelon and Goldfish crackers and counting children all day long. 1 . . . 2 . . . 3 . . . 4 . . . 5 . . . and then over again, as we snatched runaway buckets and bits of a hundred conversations in between. At the end of the day, our sandy, waterlogged children asked for ice cream and when they could be together at the beach again.

It is not about a happy ending. There will still be questions, procedures, concerns, and events that we will share in texts and nap time conversations, this friend and I. But these days of joy when nothing's perfect, but somehow everything is—they are the map points along our adventure in hope. They are the elements of remembrance that cause us to look back when we weren't sure of tomorrow—and say grace.

They are the slivers of light that illuminate the beauty of bearing one another's burdens and sharing in one another's delight.

BECAUSE WE BELONG to a God who is big enough to hold all our uncertainty and trust in His hands, this is how we can live. Sharing life together and reminding one another that hope is always worth the fight, pointing to the fact that even in the dark, there is light to be found. Being in community together means we get to be the ones who remind each other of what we know to be true. Some days we will be the reminder. Other days we will beg that someone just please, remind us.

In these "both and" seasons, we embrace the tango of joy and laughter, even as it smashes right up against pain and fear.

It is how we will always know it, until there is nothing left to fear anymore.

So for today, we wait.

We wait for tomorrow with the secret smiling hope of children who already know the next chapter of this particular story.

The chapter that whispers the truth that fear and grief will never win, and that hope is always worth the fight.

UNTIL THEN, we keep reaching for the matches. Until then, we keep lighting the candles.

ROASTED VEGETABLE TIPS

R oasted Vegetables are quite the game changer, especially if you have vegetable-squeamish children. The process is simple if you remember these four main things.

Give them space.

Give them heat.

Give them fat.

Give them seasoning.

GIVE THEM SPACE. Use two baking sheets, rather than crowding onto one. Crowding usually leads to soggy or steamed vegetables. If cooking a variety, larger pieces are better.

Give them heat. Start at a temperature of 425'F for most vegetables. Check them after ten minutes, stir, and then check again after every 7-10 minutes.

Give them fat. Extra Virgin Olive Oil is one of the best. I usually avoid using a cooking spray oil when roasting, and tend to mix them with my hands.

Give them seasoning. Salt lightly at the beginning as you can always add more, but you want to be able to taste the natural caramelization that occurs with roasting. Some of my favorite seasoning combinations are a little salt, pepper, garlic powder, and a dash of paprika.

A FEW ADDITIONAL TIPS.

Parchment paper is a helpful convenience item when roasting. Not only does it keep your veg from sticking, but you also get a pass with the dishes.

There are a few vegetables that don't often roast well with others because of their moisture; roast these separately— Mushrooms, Zucchini, Tomatoes, Eggplant to name a few.

Though the texture of fresh vegetables roasted is the very best, you can roast frozen whole green beans and butternut squash and definitely, corn.

WINTER ROOT VEGETABLE BOWL

W inter Root Vegetable Bowl
This bowl is one of texture and colorful, healthy, goodness. Fresh crisp greens, warm roasted beets and sweet potatoes, and nutty quinoa, all tossed with a light vinaigrette and then topped with toasted nuts and goat cheese. This recipe is also a wonderful make ahead meal prep option.

PROVISIONS.
2-3 red or golden beets, peeled and sliced in rounds, and then quartered
3 sweet potatoes, peeled and cubed
3/4 cup of uncooked Quinoa, rinsed
2 tsp. Chicken base
Mixed Greens 4 cups
1-2 ounces Goat Cheese, crumbled
Sliced Almonds, toasted

VINAIGRETTE.

1 fl. Ounce rice wine vinegar
4 Tbs. Good olive oil
Salt and Pepper
A small dash of maple syrup or honey, about 1/2 tsp.

METHOD.

Preheat Oven to 425'F

Whisk dressing ingredients together.

Roast potatoes and beets after tossing them with olive oil and a dash of salt & pepper. Give them plenty of space and parchment underneath them, and they will get lovely crisp edges. Set aside to cool.

Meanwhile, bring a medium pot to a boil with 1 1/2 cups water, the chicken base, and the quinoa. Once boiling, reduce the heat to a small simmer and cook for 18-20 minutes. Fluff quinoa with a fork and set aside.

Toss the greens, quinoa, and roasted veg together in a large bowl. Drizzle the dressing and then top with toasted almonds and goat cheese. Add extra cracked pepper to taste.

If you have enjoyed

FEASTING & FORAGING

please visit www.happygostuckey.com/simmer to
download your free electronic copy of

SIMMER: SIX SEASONAL SOUPS &
THE STORIES THAT INSPIRED
THEM

Let's continue the conversation
on Instagram: @happygostuckey

WITH GRATITUDE TO

Leah Janik and Lumarie Photography, for being so kind to help me dream up this little book. Your images made my recipes come to life and I am so grateful for the part you played.

Kate Motaung, for being the kind of editor every writer needs— honest with a strong sense of diplomacy and kindness.

Amanda Pierce and Birdsong Design, not only for gifting me your kitchen for three days to shoot the recipes within, but also for gifting me the design of my own lovely BlueHouse kitchen.

The Monday School Fam, for being the dearest people to walk in community with and for not minding all the salad recipes I inadvertently tested out on you. You all make Mondays sweet.

Mom, for always celebrating with me.

Lance & the Girls, for your patience, grace, and the hundred frozen pizzas you ate while I was in the writing zone. You three are the dream come true.

Made in the USA
Columbia, SC
29 October 2021